Business Competency for Lawyers

A LawBiz Management Special Report

by **Edward Poll**

Published by

LawBiz® Management Company
(a division of Edward Poll & Associates, Inc.)
421 Howland Canal
Venice, CA 90291
Phone: (800) 837-5880
Fax: (310) 578-1769
E-mail: EdPoll@LawBiz.com
Web site: www.LawBiz.com
Weblog: www.LawBizblog.com
Copyright © 2006 Edward Poll, LawBiz® Management Company,
and Edward Poll & Associates, Inc.
All Rights Reserved.

Printed in the United States of America.

Report design by Creative Quadrant, Inc.

Nothing contained in this publication is to be considered as the offering of management advice or legal advice for specific cases, and readers are responsible for obtaining such counsel from their own advisers. This publication and any forms, suggestions, or advice herein are intended for educational and informational purposes only.

Additional copies of this publication may be purchased from Edward Poll & Associates, Inc., which also produces other publications of interest to the legal and professional services communities.

Library of Congress Control Number: 2006922205

ISBN: 978-0-9654948-5-4

Table of Contents

Foreword 1

Understanding Business Competency 2
    Introduction and definition
    Importance of business competency
    The unique law firm environment

Law Firm Business Planning 8
    Service elements
    Warning signs
    The five planning steps

Law Firm Business Performance 14
    Performance factors
    Accounting methods
    Large firm performance
    Small firm performance

Cash Flow Management 20
    Collection cycle
    Statements
    Accounts management
    Clients trust accounts
    Average daily balance
    Bank sweep
    Deposits

Billing Rates and Cycles 26
    Identifying costs
    Billing options
    Value mix
    Raising fees

Collections..32
    Written engagement agreement
    Planning
    Time records
    Ancillary expenses
    Communication
    Collection service

The Junior Attorney's Impact..38
    Information metrics
    Associate value
    Financial ownership

The Client's Impact..44
    Client business essentials
    Client financial arrangements
    Client mix

Case Studies in Understanding Business Competency....................50
    The real cost of e-mail
    The real cost of lawyer turnover
    The real cost of capital investment
    The real cost of telecommuting

Business Competency Resources 56

Foreword

In the decade I've known Ed Poll, he's done more to assist attorneys in building their legal practices than anyone I know. What impresses me most is his pragmatic, direct approach. From billing rates to generating consensus among partners, Ed tackles the problems most practices ignore as they rush from client to client, attempting to stave off one crisis after another.

As a consultant, my own focus is to generate high value for clients so the return on investment is powerful and the fees, therefore, are never an issue. The legal profession, however, is far from that model—its emphasis is on billable time and hourly rates. Yet, what is great legal advice worth? What is the value of a successful defense or suit? Must law firms pursue contingency fees to overcome the limitations of hourly billing models?

In these pages, Ed explains how to set up an effective and efficient business that is worth your investment. He discusses client mix and the consequent profitability scenarios. He examines how to maximize cash flow, avoid lagging payments, and use collections services. He takes a hard look at the size and profitability of the firm to determine future success. In essence, he looks at law the way I look at consulting—as a business that must be run efficiently and profitably.

Attorneys provide legal assistance to clients, but their own practices must be run as businesses, not merely as adjuncts to the law. After all, no one can help clients properly if they, themselves, aren't strong. Read Ed's words with care—and keep this book handy on your desk, not the shelf. Don't make the mistake of failing to help your clients because you're ineffective at helping yourself. Value is in the eye of the beholder. Herein, Ed helps you develop better insight into your own value.

— *Alan Weiss, Ph.D.*
Author of Million Dollar Consulting: The Professional's Guide to Growing a Practice, *McGraw-Hill, 2002*
President, Summit Consulting Group, Inc.

Section 1:

Understanding Business Competency

Smith and Jones began their litigation partnership nearly a year ago because they had complementary practices and thought they could be more successful by combining their strengths. They soon realized that, while they were serving more clients individually and collectively, they had no real understanding of what more business meant to their combined finances. Billings, collections, budgets—they had given none of those topics much thought, and didn't know where to turn for guidance. What should they do now?

Introduction and definition

Good business judgment requires lawyers to understand the business context—for their own firm and for clients—within which legal advice is delivered. Put another way, lawyers should be *business literate*. Business competency does not involve mastering all the details of management jargon. For a lawyer, it is simply about mastering the three-part cycle that drives any business:

▸ Win the business (the sales and marketing function).

The Work Cycle

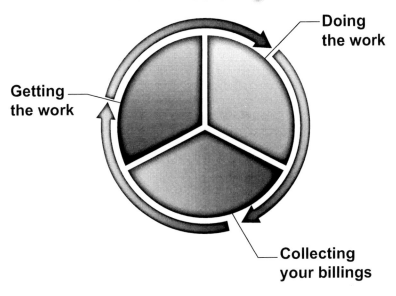

Getting the work

Doing the work

Collecting your billings

▶ Do the work as effectively and efficiently as possible (the production function).

▶ Get paid (the collections function, which is inseparable from basic finance).

These three functions are distinct and separate. Most lawyers are familiar and capable in the sales and production function, but they do themselves a disservice by handling the collection function personally: The client who owes money is uncertain whether the lawyer is calling for production or collection reasons, and likely will not call back at all. However, for the lawyer personally, understanding the process of getting paid is the core of necessary business competency.

The business-competent lawyer understands the

---

operation of the firm as a business (budget, collections, profit, loss), the firm's billing structure, how each attorney determines firm profitability, and the importance of clients and their own businesses. This LawBiz special report addresses such basic business facts. It is not intended to be a comprehensive or technical treatment of the subject. Instead, it is a practical starting point to help attorneys understand the essential ways in which their practice is a business as well as a profession.

Importance of business competency

Running a law firm in a businesslike way improves the professionalism of the practice of law. The purpose is not simply to get more money for the lawyer; it also benefits the client. A profitable law practice is much more likely to avoid such ethical problems as dipping into client trust accounts, either as direct fraud or as a stopgap "loan." Moreover, a law firm run as a business will also approach client service more efficiently—returning phone calls promptly, creating and adhering to a budget, providing sufficient details on clients' invoices, etc. You can't truly be a professional service business until you understand The Business of Law®.

Business competency and the unique law firm environment

All organizations, large and small, law firms and non-law firms, have one thing in common: a finite limit to discretionary spending.

► Non-discretionary (mandatory) spending is that spending required by your current structure and by law: debt obligations, insurance, Social Security and federal income tax payments.

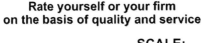

Business Competency

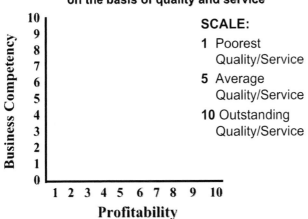

Rate yourself or your firm
on the basis of quality and service

SCALE:

1 Poorest
Quality/Service

5 Average
Quality/Service

10 Outstanding
Quality/Service

Business Competency (vertical axis: 10 9 8 7 6 5 4 3 2 1 0)

Profitability (horizontal axis: 1 2 3 4 5 6 7 8 9 10)

- Adjustable spending is that spending that is important but can be modified (such as lease terms and staffing).

- Discretionary spending is that spending that could be prevented if you had to.

What is unique to law firms is the impact so many individuals have directly on spending. In many law firms, individual partners, even lawyers generally, have the ability to direct discretionary resource consumption, from purchasing new office furniture to charging the firm with personal meals and travel. Instilling business competency is a way to control this spending, run the firm more professionally, and make it more financially successful.

All law firms must provide value to their clients. And they must be profitable in order to open their doors the following day. The firms whose attorneys understand these two truths in the context of business competency will ensure their long-term future and success.

"Law is not a profession at all, but rather a business service station and repair shop."

—Adlai E. Stevenson, Senator

Section 2:

Law Firm Business Planning

Smith handled a large volume of cases for individuals: small claims, disputes with landlords, wrongful dismissal suits. Jones had a growing practice in commercial litigation for small businesses. Many of the matters they handled involved similar issues, but Smith was nervous about the way Jones relied on a relatively few large clients, while Jones worried that Smith couldn't really predict who would engage his services and when. They both realized that, if their practices continued to grow without coordination, they could be conflicted out of helping each other. What should they do now?

B usinesses fail because the owners fail to focus their energy on the business; most business owners are technicians, not entrepreneurs, according to Michael E. Gerber, best-selling author of *The E-Myth Revisited*. Law is a business as well as a profession; in order to succeed, lawyers must act in a businesslike way. But Gerber may be right when it comes to lawyers. They tend to be technicians who want to do what they love doing, whether it's negotiating, drafting a contract, litigating, or some other task. They don't want to run a business, they don't

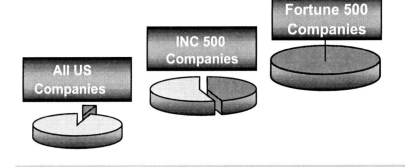

All US Companies

INC 500 Companies

Fortune 500 Companies

want to spend time seeking new clients, and they especially don't want to do business planning.

As famed UCLA basketball coach John Wooden said, "Failing to plan is planning to fail." Or as it says in Proverbs, "A people without a vision will perish." Or as Yogi Berra said, "When you come to a fork in the road, take it."

Service elements

The planning process is the business owner's job, although the technical tasks may be the medium of interaction between the business and the customer. In order to exceed the expectations of clients, lawyers must plan their businesses to include service elements and procedures that will encourage consistently high standards of client interaction, such as the following:

▶ Establish a return phone call policy. Return or have an assistant return clients' phone calls within two to four hours.

- Know your clients' concerns and understand their business.

- Create a client-friendly office environment. Have informative literature in the waiting room, and make sure it's available in languages that reflect your client's primary languages.

- Prepare your clients for interactive events such as negotiation sessions, depositions, and testimony so they know what to expect and are prepared for what might happen.

- Generate billing statements that are easy to understand and clearly list actions taken on the client's behalf during the previous month. (Keep in mind that clients want to pay for value received, not for time expended, even if time is the unit of measurement.)

- Regularly ask clients for feedback about whether they are pleased with your services.

Warning signs

Most lawyers begin to realize that they are in trouble only after the money ceases to come in the door. However, cash flow cessation is usually the last symptom of a downward spiral that started long before.

An example of warning signs can be taken from the world of sports: a law practice is like an athlete who is exercising in hot weather. Hydration—maintaining adequate body fluids—is critical to an athlete's performance and health. In fact, dehydration can lead to serious medical problems

Everyone Plans

…some in their head and some in writing.

- CEOs of smaller businesses usually carry the information in their heads.
- CEOs of larger companies usually have it in writing and communicate it to others.
- Smaller businesses fail at a much higher rate than larger companies.

Is there a correlation?

such as heat exhaustion, heat stroke, and ultimately death. Unfortunately, the body's ability to detect dehydration is slow. There is a lag between the time the body becomes dehydrated and when it sends the thirst signal to head to the nearest water supply to do something about it. Knowledgeable athletes anticipate this problem by drinking plenty of fluids before and during exercise, even if they are not thirsty.

A law practice works the same way. The point when cash stops coming in the door is much too late to start wondering if there is a problem. The seeds of the problem were undoubtedly sown weeks, months, or even years earlier. Like the overheated athlete, lawyers need to think about the business side of the practice before they run into problems.

 Planning is important not only for cash flow but also when dealing with a banker about a loan. Bankers normally request a business plan in order to facilitate a loan. Even if you have "challenges" in your business, you need to address them in a plan. The plan does not need to be complex, but it should be developed as the result of an organized process.

The five planning steps

1. Prepare and agree to the plan.

In a law firm, it is important that all of the key players agree on the direction of the firm. If the partners are not clear about the overall goals as well as specific objectives and strategies, then the planning process is bound to be sabotaged and of little use. Partners need to "buy in" to a plan. Solos are not immune from this requirement either. They must get a spouse or "significant other" to accept the general direction of the firm. That is why the first element of any plan is to agree to make and abide by the plan. The starting point is to gather historical information about the firm's business performance, analyze it and develop realistic modifications for the future. This involves marketing and financial data in the form of documents, statistics, reports, survey results, and, when there is nothing else, educated guesses. All this data will create a snapshot of the firm's current marketing and economic health.

2. Identify goals.

A firm that does not decide what kind of practice it wants will wind up with one reflecting whatever walks in the door. It is doubtful that serendipity and whim are the best paths to success. Set professional and personal objectives and stick to them.

3. Create the marketing plan.

Since any practice is dependent on clients, getting and keeping the clients is critical to your success. A marketing plan helps you to see who these elusive people are and how to attract them to your door. Create a profile of your ideal client and develop a marketing strategy that focuses on this target, not on everyone. You can increase your revenue dramatically by focusing on clients who will give you the work that you want.

4. Create the financial plan.

The financial plan is the culmination of all the earlier information gathering, thinking, and planning. The financial plan is the statement, in financial or monetary terms (the language of business), of individual and firm objectives and goals.

5. Evaluate and revise the plan.

Good planning is not static; it is meant to be a guide against which to judge actions or outcomes. If a certain aspect of a plan is not working or needs some adjustment, change it. The beauty of a flexible plan is that it can be revised to better reflect the reality of changing situations to produce the desired outcome. Planning is an ongoing process.

Section 3:

Law Firm Business Performance

Smith and Jones figured that complex accounting wasn't necessary to run a small firm. They anticipated keeping a simple running tally of receipts and expenses by month. Then they started to realize that they didn't just have billed work—some was completed and not yet billed, some was billed but not yet collected. And they realized it just as some major expenses for taxes and malpractice coverage were due. They weren't sure they had enough cash in hand to pay these special expenses plus the regular monthly bills. What should they do now?

Performance factors

The firm's performance generates profitability through the interaction of these fundamental factors:

▸ Revenue, whether tracked by attorney, practice area or office

▸ Billing rates, whether hourly, blended (an average), fixed fee or other measure

▸ Utilization, the percentage of a workweek (usually expressed as an annual average) that a lawyer actually bills

Collected-to-Billed Ratio

Above 95%: Are your rates too low?

Below 80%: It's a recipe for trouble.

- Realization, the amount of time actually billed and collected

- Leverage, defined as the ratio of non-partners (associates, paralegals, staff) to partners

- Expenses, related to both operations and compensation, as a percent of revenues

- Collection rate, the speed at which billable work is turned into cash receipts

In the simplest of terms, profit can be determined by taking the total annual gross revenue by client and subtracting the costs associated with serving that client, including how long the firm has to wait for the payments. Billing rates and realization percentage are key markers of any firm's financial strength. Try looking at your standard rates and at your blended average billing rates by category of timekeeper. Are you able to bill premium rates? Must you frequently offer discounts? How do your rates compare to those of your competitors? The answers can be revealing.

Realization is sometimes discussed in two levels:

- Percent of billable or booked hours billed (billed-to-billable ratio).

- Percent of billed work collected (collected-to-billed ratio).

The goal is to have a high collected to billable ratio. An overall financial ratio of less than 80% to 85% is a recipe for trouble. An overall ratio of greater than 95% may mean your rates are too low—clients could be paying quickly because the amounts are not burdensome to them.

Accounting methods

There are two basic methods for keeping track of law firm financial performance: accrual versus cash accounting. Accrual records reflect income irrespective of whether cash has been collected. In other words, accrual accounting reflects billings, work in progress (completed but not yet billed) and accounts receivable (work billed but not yet collected). Cash accounting, on the other hand, reflects only collections, never billings or work in progress. Almost all small law firms operate on a cash basis, accounting for cash as it comes in and goes out. Larger law firms maintain both cash and accrual records.

Income statements, also called profit and loss or P&L statements, tell how well a firm did financially in a given period of time. Income statements use the accrual method to tell how much revenue has been billed, how much expense has been accrued, and how much net income or profit resulted. Income or profit figures generally have little relevance to small law firms. Small professional service firms typically operate on a cash basis, with the lawyer's salary or draw coming from positive cash flow.

Large firm performance

The fundamental measurement of financial performance at most large law firms is net income, or profit per partner. This is publicly reported in *The American Lawyer*'s "AmLaw 100" annual list of the largest U.S. law firms. Profits per partner for these firms has soared in recent years, with nearly half reporting levels of $1 million or more per partner. Many of these are large New York City firms, but geography has become less important as a profit determiner. Profits-per-partner eclipsed the $1 million level in 2004 at six firms either headquartered or originally started in Los Angeles. In 2000, not one L.A. firm reached that level. Why have all these large law firms experienced such increases in profits? The answer is multi-fold:

▸ Increased focus on cost-cutting

▸ Reduction in equity partners' ranks (with increased number of income or contract partners)

▸ Alternative value or contingency engagement agreements where the law firms benefited by outstanding results

▸ Substantial growth in clients and/or clients' legal needs.

Small firm performance

For the smaller practitioner, the analysis of profitability determinants is simpler because it is based on cash flow. Financial analysis is a process of identifying and deducting the expenses of the practice from monthly cash received. Fixed expenses typically include:

▶ Staff, including salaries and taxes

▶ Occupancy (rent, taxes, utilities)

▶ Equipment (including depreciation)

▶ Malpractice insurance

▶ Outside professional services

The largest single expense that should be variable is the partner or shareholder's draw or salary. This reflects the lawyer's personal needs and style of living, and the most sensible practice is to increase it only as the firm's performance produces sufficient income to do so. Amounts set aside for savings and retirement should be approached similarly to salary.

All of this is dependent on revenue, which for a small practice can be variable. A good method for estimating it is the accounting measure of turnover ratio: accounts receivable balance divided by the result of billings per days in the billing period (either monthly or annually). The turnover ratio tells a lawyer to expect payment for billings X number of days after a client receives a statement. The national average for law firms, according to one survey, is between 120 and 150 days — as much as five months. That means that a typical small firm should have funds sufficient to operate for at least six months without new billings coming in. The lesson: Cash flow and collections are the crucial determinants of business performance.

The largest single expense that should be variable is the partner or shareholder's draw or salary.

Section 4:

Cash Flow Management

Smith completed a successful month with over 160 billable hours. One quarter of those were for settling a will contest, and they would cover some big upcoming expenses. Smith wanted to send the bill on the first of the month, and made a courtesy phone call to say it was coming. He got no answer at home and tried the client's office—where an assistant said the client had left on a three-month European trip. There was no way to get payment for the 40 billable hours that Smith had been counting on. What should he do now?

Understanding cash flow is essential to business competency. The cash-flow statement can have many names: a cash-flow budget, a statement of cash or a forecast. Whatever the moniker, this statement is important for review on at least a weekly, if not daily, basis. It is the single most important tool for the success of any business activity.

Many office expense items cannot be controlled or reduced once set in place. However, some expenses, such as rent, can be modified given the right circumstances. It is possible to negotiate a reduction of the rent schedule with your landlord. Other savings items could include:

- ▸ Library expenditures (you can share a library or use your county law library)

An alternative to monthly billing: Bill ¼ of your clients each week

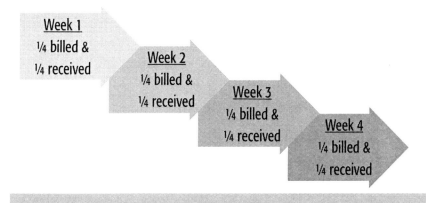

Week 1
¼ billed &
¼ received

Week 2
¼ billed &
¼ received

Week 3
¼ billed &
¼ received

Week 4
¼ billed &
¼ received

- Payroll (to a more limited extent if a sole practitioner)

- Dues and subscriptions

Savings in these three areas alone can be substantial. Further, if you know when to anticipate low- and high-cash-flow periods, you can postpone, advance or finance equipment purchases.

Effective cash flow management often comes down to the steps any lawyer can take to get funds into the bank account as quickly as possible. Often these are commonsense efficiencies that, over time, can make a tremendous difference.

Nine Steps to Greater Control

1. Manage your collection cycle.

Develop alternatives to diversify your receivables stream—for example, by billing one-fourth of the alphabet each week. You'll receive money from one-fourth of your clients weekly, rather than once per month. This evens out your receipt of cash over the month. You could also shorten your monthly billing cycle, sending out invoices on or about the 25th of the month so that clients receive statements on or before the first day of the following month. Since most people pay their bills on or about the first of the month, a bill that comes after that is frequently kept for payment until the following month.

2. Send statements after a particularly beneficial psychological event.

If you bill when clients are happy because you've won a motion or negotiated a favorable deal—even if somewhat before or beyond the normal billing date—they're more likely to pay quickly. Such billing places the client on the peak of the "satisfaction curve," the time of least resistance for payment of fees. Later, the client will invariably forget how important you were in the process of the result and wonder why the bill is so high. Once in that state of mind, the statement for services will sit unpaid until some future date.

3. "Age" your accounts receivable once a week.

Determine which clients are behind on their payments, even if you have been working on other matters. Forgetting or ignoring "old" clients results in forgetting or ignoring the accounts receivable. This results in the failure to collect your money. Remembering old open accounts is vital. On one hand, you will be able to pursue collection with the regular, weekly reminders that money is owed to you. On the other hand, you will be able to thank a client who has paid, the kind of courtesy that pays off in increased goodwill.

4. Use trust accounts effectively.

Flat fees or retainers can be withdrawn from a client's trust account as specified in the engagement agreement. Withdrawal can be predicated upon reaching specific events: a date certain, the filing of a complaint, the signing of a settlement or merger agreement. **Even retainer fees can be deposited into a general account** if the agreement says that the retainer is not for future work but for the lawyer specifically being engaged (and thus taken off the market). Some lawyers will **split the fee,** making part of it a non-refundable retainer and placing the balance into the trust account for withdrawal as the work is performed. **This method makes a clear distinction between the two elements, again as specified by an event or date** which triggers a withdrawal from the trust account and places it into the general account. This avoids waiting for the client to say "yes" after the fact and allows you to get the money sooner

5. Maintain a high average daily balance.

Most banks calculate the "average daily balance" in your bank account. This is one of the most significant bits of information with which a bank works in analyzing a loan request. Thus, you want to maintain as high a balance as possible. This can be done either by keeping a large sum of money in the bank or by keeping limited funds in the account for a longer period of time. You can keep funds in the account longer by depositing revenue immediately upon receipt and spreading the payment of bills throughout the month. Do not pay your bills all at one time: This will cause an exaggerated dip in your account balance rather than provide an even flow of funds.

6. Don't wait to deposit checks.

This is the first rule of cash flow management. Too many catastrophic events can happen while a check is awaiting deposit. The client may, in the interim, become angry, for whatever reason, and stop payment on the check. The check may reach your client's bank at a time when the account is overdrawn. The client may have been named as a defendant in a lawsuit for which attachment procedures are available. Because of this, the client's bank account may be "marked" for a sum large enough to cause the presentation of the check you are holding to be rejected. In each of these cases, a check that had been deposited immediately would have cleared the client's bank and been credited to your account.

7. Consider an automatic bank sweep.

Banks provide for an "automatic sweep" on a daily basis. Establish a minimum amount of money, such as $2,500, to remain in your general account. The exact sum depends on the amount of checks and deposits that pass through your bank account each month. Then, instruct the bank to segregate all funds in excess of this amount at the end of each day and "sweep" or transfer those "excess" funds into a money market (interest bearing) account until needed. The bank can also be instructed to call you, or to automatically transfer funds into the general account from the money market account, in the event the balance goes below the established minimum amount.

8. Negotiate immediate access to deposits.

Some banks place a "hold" on funds deposited with them until the funds have cleared through the banking system. This may be as long as seven days. However, you can negotiate with the bank so that you have immediate access to your deposited funds.

9. Deposit all checks from clients.

Do this even if the amount received does not match the amount due per the statement. Make a photocopy of the check. After making the deposit, call the client and ask for an explanation of the difference. You will ultimately reconcile the amount paid with the amount due; however, in the meantime, you will have deposited and benefited from the amount sent to you. The only exception is when there is a disputed claim, and a check is marked "paid in full" with the check amount being less than the amount owed to you.

Section 5:

Billing Rates and Cycles

Jones felt that his good work for his largest client, an auto dealership, justified a fee increase. Then the dealership's owner called. It had been a tough couple of months for him. He had more collections work for Jones, but asked Jones for a 10% hourly rate reduction—unless Jones could give him a flat monthly fee for all his collections work. Jones had no idea how much average time he put in on collection matters, and whether he could afford to do what his biggest client asked. What should he do now?

Today most lawyers are paid by the hour. But lawyers don't really sell time; they sell solutions. Their goal should be providing value: advice that means solutions to the client. Until well into the post-World War II era, legal fees were based not only on time spent, but also the nature of the service, the result achieved and the amount at stake. Charging an appropriate legal fee was a matter of professional judgment. That changed in the mid-1960s when clients began demanding detailed billing statements and lawyers used time records as a management tool to seek greater efficiencies. Today, most lawyers are paid by the hour—almost in the same way as an hourly laborer. Our billings are "features" lists: this is what I did, this is the time I worked and this is what

Address value and benefits: the worth—as opposed to the cost—of the service.

you owe me. That approach breeds dissatisfaction among clients, because it doesn't address value and benefits— the worth, as opposed to the cost, of the service.

Identifying costs

Attorneys can use a business competency understanding to make a market assessment of whether their rates are too high—or too low. Once you understand the marketplace of your client's needs, you can better assess the value you provide, and better reflect it in your bills. A simple checklist can help identify the elements to consider:

► Goals to be achieved

► Current status of the project or case

► Complexity of the project or case

► Number of parties involved

► Client's budget for this matter

► Documents to be generated (drafting responsibility and expected number of drafts)

► Extent of travel anticipated

► Extent of work to be done by in-house and outside counsel respectively

► Extent of expected negotiations/discovery

► Staffing plan

Assess billing options for value rendered

Most firms use such an analysis to determine the mix of hourly rates used to accomplish the work. However, almost any case or project can be broken into tasks and each task can be priced separately and differently, to create multiple pricing schemes within a single transaction based on client preferences and value perceptions. Different clients can be approached differently. Creating a matrix can demonstrate to clients those areas where costs can be controlled and where costs are inherent, and educate clients about what can be done to lower the overall cost of a project. Below is one example of such a matrix applied to an acquisition transaction. It shows various steps in the process, and whether they could be billed at the hourly rate of each attorney, a blend or average of all hourly rates, a fixed price, or a percentage of the transaction value.

Tasks	Pricing Options			
	Hourly	Blended Hourly	Fixed Cost	Agreed % Option
Letter of intent	X		X	
Draft preliminary purchase and sale agreement	X		X	
Negotiations	X			X
Final draft agreement and site agreements	X	X		
Due diligence	X	X	X	X
Closing	X			
Post-closing agenda	X	X	X	
	X = possible pricing options			

Change the value mix

Such value-added elements will let you generate billing statements that are easy to understand and that clearly list actions taken on the client's behalf while relating them to the time it took to realize that value. These billing statements will be more meaningful to the client, and will go beyond a mere laundry list of tasks performed.

However, even if lawyers are providing and documenting value, price pressures can lead clients, particularly corporate ones, to ask for lower billing rates. Value billing does not remove the pressure from clients on fees. The advantage of charging for value, however, is that, rather than lowering the price, lawyers are in a position to take value/services off the table in order to deliver a lower price to the client. In effect, when the client wants a reduced price, unbundle the services to accomplish that objective. You are charging a different price for a different group of tasks and functions.

In other words, for X dollars, you as a lawyer will do this and for "Y" dollars you will do that less "abc." While "abc" may not be important, the client gets the message that you're **adjusting the price to fit the appropriate level based on the service to be delivered.** For example, consider the components of an hourly fee. If returned phone calls within 2 hours are part of your regular hourly rate, take that response time off the table if you lower your hourly rate in response to your client's request. Tell the client that your response time will be 24, or even 48, hours. The point will be clear: You're not lowering your price, you're changing the value composition of what the client is buying.

> **"Clients want service more than they want their lawyers to be competent or fair with fees."**
>
> *—Understanding Your Clients, Barbara Curran,*
> *American Bar Foundation Study, 1982*

Raising fees

Turn to the positive. Although lawyers are often uncomfortable about raising their rates, you can soften the blow of a fee increase by adding value to your service. In other words, do more things that cost less than the increase. If you handle estate planning, for example, you could add financial planning as a service, either as part of the fee package or for a designated added fee. Sometimes, showing that you provide better-than-excellent service is all you need to justify a fee increase. For example, consider packaging final documents in an attractive folder and hand-delivering them to the client. This improved presentation adds only pennies to your costs, but it will be perceived as an example of your caring for and nurturing the client. Faster turnaround from engagement to completion is another way of adding value and exceeding expectations.

Section 6:

Collections

Jones referred to Smith a business client who owned a machine shop. The client was buying a new home and needed help with the closing. Smith devoted considerable time to a complicated tax issue, and billed accordingly. The client objected, saying he was entitled to a discount because of all the work he had given Jones. Smith had taken on the closing based on a handshake with a client who refused to return calls. And the next time Jones sent his own bill to the client, it came back marked "Return to Sender." What should they do now?

S everal years ago, when the 300-lawyer global law firm of Altheimer & Gray was forced to file for bankruptcy, a very important fact got little attention: The firm had $30 million in outstanding accounts receivable. Had Altheimer & Gray been more diligent and aggressive at collecting the money it was owed, it might have remained alive. Other law firms have had similar experiences. Steve Finley, founder of Finley Kumble (generally credited with being the first megafirm before it disintegrated in the late 1980s), contended that the firm's demise began with a new managing partner who was not so aggressive about collecting receivables as Kumble had been.

The importance of collecting the money you are owed could

> **The truth is that a lawyer's inventory is not billable hours—it's the cash those hours represent.**

not be more obvious, for the largest law firms and for solo practitioners alike. And yet, this lesson is hard for lawyers to grasp, because they think financial success means ever rising billable hours. The truth is that a lawyer's inventory is not billable hours—it's the cash those hours represent. Some lawyers may feel that emphasizing receivables is unprofessional, but the Internal Revenue Code says that unless you bill under an accrual system, you can never have the tax benefit of writing off bad debts.

Generating enough new work to cover bad debts simply isn't the answer. Depending on your firm and the type of work you do, the ramp-up time from first client contact to first assignment can take up to 18 months. And the average billing cycle for new work is typically 120 days—making it nearly two years before you see a return on your initial efforts.

The better course for any lawyer is to get clients who know they must pay their bills, and to make sure the clients do so within 60 to 90 days. That means a businesslike approach to the issue of collecting money, as outlined by these eight steps.

1. Get it in writing.

The rules of professional conduct generally require

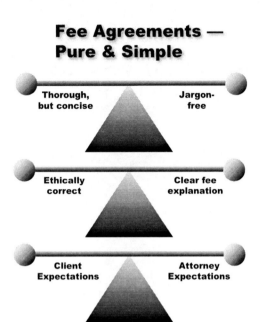

Fee Agreements — Pure & Simple

Thorough, but concise — Jargon-free

Ethically correct — Clear fee explanation

Client Expectations — Attorney Expectations

that lawyers have a signed engagement letter for a new client, stating each party's responsibilities for making the engagement a success. You will unquestionably have an easier time collecting your fee if you get it incorporated in the engagement letter—not so much the terms of enforcement as making sure clients understand that they're entering a two-way relationship. The lawyer agrees to perform to the best of his or her ability in accord with professional standards, and the client agrees to communicate and cooperate fully—which includes paying the bill.

2. Make a plan.

In addition to a fee agreement for a given engagement, prepare a budget that attempts to determine, to the extent possible, what will happen. If it is litigation, budget to the best of your ability for the nature and extent of the pleadings to be filed, the number and complexity of depositions you will have, how long you think it's going to take you to prepare, what you expect the other side to do, and so forth. The budget should thus address events, time and money, and you should get your client to buy into and accept it. When you do that, your chances of collecting your fee go up significantly because the client understands what to expect and has participated in the analysis.

3. Keep accurate time records.

Studies have shown that unless lawyers record and bill their time as they proceed through the day, there is a minimum 10% to 15% loss of revenue. One of the newest and most insidious contributors to lost billable time is e-mail. Like phone conversations, communication by e-mail on client matters represents billable time. Yet lawyers are going so fast, doing so many things simultaneously (sometimes called multitasking), that they don't actually write down their time notation as they're working on e-mails. And if they don't do it then, by the end of the day, let alone the end of the week, they're going to forget how much time was involved. The importance of client e-mails is lost, and so too is profitability through incomplete billing.

4. Minimize ancillary expenses.

Even if your agreement with a client lets you charge for opening a file on each matter or for photocopying a file before giving it to a client on request, consider whether these or other charges will ultimately cost more money than they bring in. If other firms in your position aren't doing the

> **Clients get angry at their attorneys for "nickel and diming" on charges they consider overhead and part of the cost of doing business, especially with what they perceive to be very high hourly fees they pay to lawyers.**

same thing, you may stand out and lose a client or prospect. Clients get angry at their attorneys for "nickel and diming" on charges they consider overhead and part of the cost of doing business, especially with what they perceive to be very high hourly fees they pay to lawyers.

5. Communicate constantly.

If clients have the ability to pay but are not paying, my experience is they're unhappy with some aspect of the representation. They choose to express that by slowing down or stopping the payment schedule. To avoid such a situation, stay in continual touch with the client about progress according to the budget. Make note of any additional time and expenses that may be incurred. If a slowdown in payments does take place and you suspect it may be due to client dissatisfaction, talk with the client and find out what the issue is.

6. Don't ask for money yourself.

If payment hasn't arrived, I advise lawyers not to be the ones to call the clients about it. Instead, ask someone from your staff who's good with people and sensitive to their needs to make the call. If the lawyer calls, clients may become confused about whether the call is for the purpose of requesting information, seeking new business, or requesting payment. Don't confuse the client. The best practice is to keep yourself apart from the collections function.

7. If necessary, use a collection service.

There are certainly ethical snares involved, but you can avoid them by disclosing to a collection service only those details that are absolutely necessary for them to do their job without jeopardizing client confidentiality. Moreover, it is a given that a collection effort should not be made unless you have reviewed the client file and made sure that there is no evidence of negligence on your part.

8. Walk away when necessary.

The old expression that you can't get blood out of a turnip remains valid. Ultimately a non-collection situation may come down either to working out terms with a client who is willing but unable to pay, or walking away from the engagement. In fact, in most cases, you have a right to withdraw if you see the account receivable growing and client payments slowing. When things reach the point where payment appears unlikely, that right becomes an obligation.

Section 7:

The Junior Attorney's Impact

Smith and Jones felt they could justify adding an associate. Their choice, fresh out of law school, did good work—so good that after three months she requested a salary increase. When Smith and Jones pointed out that the associate's output was actually down during the latest month due to time spent in CLE training, the associate replied that the training made her more valuable, justifying more pay—and threatened to quit if she didn't receive it. Smith and Jones faced losing both their help and the benefit of training they paid for. What should they do now?

Despite being called partnerships (or LLPs or PCs), the governance of large law firms has fallen to a very few in the organization ("the management committee"). This tends to create a corporate-style environment in which most attorneys tend to see themselves as employees, not actual or potential owners. This has a big impact on business competency. As law firms become more corporate, dissemination of key financial benchmarks within the partnership, and the firm's lawyers generally, tends to become more restricted.

$$\text{Billings} - \frac{\left[\text{Associate's Total Compensation} + \text{Direct and Indirect Expenses}\right]}{} = \text{Net Profit}$$

Information metrics

Any lawyer who has more than a solo practice should consider this list of key metrics, then ask how many of them you know for your firm:

- Gross revenues
- Net revenues
- Revenue per partner
- Revenue per lawyer
- Profits per partner
- Number of new clients per year
- Total number of matters now active
- New matters per year
- Client retention and loss rates
- Total billable hours
- Cost of a billable hour
- Billed hours
- Realization rates

Estimates on the first five metrics appear annually in print for the largest firms. Otherwise, few attorneys in large firms have access to all the data. More to the point, how many partners, even if they had access, would possess the business competency to calculate, or even understand, the traditional key measures of law firm performance: realization, utilization, leverage and expenses? How many know, or understand, the firm's collection rate—or their own personal one?

And if partners are in such a position, why expect different from the firm's associates—potential partners of the future? Laments about the lack of associate loyalty are less frequent these days than at the height of the dot-com boom, but turnover is still much higher than a decade ago. I suspect that much of that is due to a lack of information and understanding of a firm's financials, and how they apply to each lawyer.

Earlier sections discussed how various factors in partners' performance affect the firm's efficiency and profitability. But since associates also play a role in the firm's bottom line, let's look here at the junior lawyer's impact on profits as well. Remember, *every* lawyer in the firm has an impact on the business's success.

Associate value

Associates should realize that they cannot and will not remain with their firm unless it is profitable for the firm to keep them—if not for every month, then on an annualized basis. While the new, high-priced associates may not earn more than they cost the firm in the beginning, at some point that situation must change. In fact, large-firm managing partners agree that it takes, on average, from three to five years to break even on the investment in a new lawyer.

Ideally, the information should be available for associates to educate themselves in The Business

Whether they [associates] are owners and employers in *name,* they can become so in *behavior*—and the firm definitely benefits.

of Law®, determining their own P&L in order to determine and enhance their worth to the firm. The information to do that would include:

- Their billable hours, for the latest month and year to date

- How many hours the firm billed out for them, versus a markdown or write-off for some of the work (individually or as an average percentage applied to all associates)

- Direct expenses for compensation (including bonus and benefits) for the lawyer and his or her direct clerical help, office space (cost per square foot of the real estate directly attributable to the lawyer and his/her direct help), etc.

- Indirect expenses, or overhead (the percentage of revenue that the firm assigns on a per-attorney average to cover the cost for insurance, utilities, technology, entertainment and education, and other such expenses needed to keep the doors open)

The result should determine an individual net profit value to the firm: Billings - [Associate's Total Compensation + Direct and Indirect Expenses] = Net Profit.

Financial ownership

The net is the profit available resulting from an associate's effort. This is the bottom line in determining young lawyers' value to the firm. Few associates at large firms have access to the numbers for this calculation, though with a little effort they could probably learn enough to make an educated estimate. Fewer still would be interested in doing it. If these lawyers become "partners," they will lack a sense of either management or financial ownership.

When analyzing the value of a partner to a firm, management will frequently talk about "realization." Realization focuses on collected billings, not just billing statements sent out. Normally, an associate will not have any power to deal with a client directly to collect billings. Since the firm generally selects the client, it should be its responsibility to collect the fees.

The associate's responsibility is to do the work assigned in the most effective and efficient way possible and in the shortest amount of time. Fulfilling this responsibility in a way that produces net profits for the firm is a near-guarantee to keeping an associate's job. And it will prepare the firm for the business challenges of the future.

Associates, and indeed *all* lawyers today, need to be more sensitive to the financial needs and operation of the firm. The necessary conditions for this to happen are increased openness with financial information, and better training in using it. Far too many firm meeting "numbers presentations" generally are abstract and pro forma. If the presentation is at the personal level, and the means for understanding is there, the chances are better that   the lawyers hearing it will understand why they need to be concerned about the firm's financial health and their part in the process. Whether they are owners and employers in name, they can become so in behavior—and the firm definitely benefits.

Section 8:

The Client's Impact

Smith and Jones had been marketing their services to the owner of a hardware store chain, who finally invited both of them to his office for an interview. He had plenty of business and personal matters for both attorneys to handle, but he insisted that all his communication with the attorneys should be online–via extranet, electronic billing, voice-over-Internet phone protocols. Smith and Jones would face a big expense to land the client, but didn't want to lose him after pursuing him so hard. What should they do now?

To this point, the emphasis on financial competency has been on the essentials of the firm itself. However, without our clients we have no reason to exist as lawyers. Our profession would be obsolete. No lawyer can claim business competency without understanding the business essentials of a client, and without clearly defining the importance and parameters of clients in the firm's business equation.

Client business essentials

Many lawyers never take the time, or have the business competency, to do a little digging and try to understand their clients' businesses. Clients will expect the legal

advice they receive to reflect a comprehension of their business. You don't need to be an accountant, but for top clients you should ask:

► What are their products and services?

► Who do they provide them to?

► Who are their biggest competitors?

► What are their annual revenues and profitability?

► If they are publicly traded, where are they listed and how many shares do they have?

► How many employees do they have, and where are they located?

► How much debt do they have, and when is it due?

If a lawyer cannot answer these questions about a major client, the client will soon realize and likely resent it, with possible loss of significant revenue through lack of basic business competency.

Client financial arrangements

Lawyers should have a signed engagement letter for a new client, stating each party's responsibilities for making the engagement a success. The foundation for collecting a client's fee can be created in the engagement letter by defining the responsibilities and scope of the lawyer's work and the client's obligations to pay for it. Lawyer and client must agree to all financial essentials, including:

1. The fee to be charged and how it will be calculated

2. Budgeting and staffing

3. When the fee is to be paid

4. The client's responsibilities, including payment in accord with the agreement

5. The consequences of non-payment, including the lawyer's right to withdraw

Stipulating payment rates and terms up front is the best way to get paid. If the client says at this point, "You're too expensive," you respond by saying that other of your clients find that their investment in their matters with you are more than justified by the results. However, you can understand this client's feeling and that this client should find other counsel because your fees are not negotiable. Often, this produces one of two results: (1) The client is impressed with your negotiation skills and wants to be represented by a tough, expensive lawyer, and therefore will accept your terms of engagement; or (2) The client leaves but becomes a great walking advertisement for you, convincing listeners that you must be highly qualified because you're aggressive, expensive and unapologetic.

Lawyers can also be more flexible and counter a price concern, not by lowering rates, but by taking services "off the table." In other words, for X dollars, you will do this and for "Y" dollars you will do that less "abc." The client gets the message that you are not changing your price, you are charging a different price for a different quality of service. If returned phone calls within two hours are part of your regular hourly rate, tell the client that your response time will be 24 hours at a lower price. When you get agreement on things like this up front, your chances of collecting your fee go up significantly because the client understands what to expect. The time to make it clear is right at the start—as documented in the engagement letter.

Client mix

A statistical premise called the Pareto Principle holds that, over time, most results are produced by only a few causes, generally in a proportion of 80 to 20. When applied to law firm marketing, this produces the conventional wisdom that 80% of a typical firm's revenue is produced by 20% of its clients—the large, heavy hitters. The loss of a large client is such a major risk that you may want to consider one of the most important axioms of business: make sure no single client exceeds 10% of your total revenue. Thus, if any one client "forgets" to pay you, or even leaves, the loss won't be so hard to handle. I have seen too many firms focus on a very few, larger clients and be severely damaged when the fees from that client fail to continue—from dissatisfaction, change of billing attorney, merger, recession, or other unanticipated problems.

Some firms believe that having numerous small clients leads to greater revenue stability. However, studies suggest that small clients disproportionately drain the resources of law firms while providing a disproportionately small contribution to firm profits. I am all in favor of seeking larger clients with more money and more interesting challenges. This effort, however, must be balanced to assure that the firm doesn't wind up with only a few clients, large though they may be, who put the firm at risk if they should leave.

You may be willing to accept this risk for the short-term with the intent of getting more clients so that the percentage allocation to the "larger" client is reduced while maintaining the billings at the same level for the client.

If so, make no long-term capital or other expenditures at the behest of larger clients without some type of assurance that their business will stay with you until at least the amortization for the new expenditure is completed. Otherwise a long-term strategy based exclusively on fewer, larger clients will almost always lead to disaster.

Section 9:

Case Studies in Understanding Business Competency

Jones believed that starting a blog would be a great way for both he and Smith to market their practices. He had done some reading, and it seemed easy and inexpensive. They bought the appropriate software and split the amount of time to do postings. At the end of the first month each had spent two hours a week working on the blog. At their current hourly rates, the time for blog maintenance would cost Smith and Jones thousands of dollars a year. Yet they believed the blog was a valuable marketing tool. What should they do now?

Case Study: The real cost of e-mail

Given the rapidity of response that e-mails encourage, it's likely that very few lawyers are truly capturing the time that they're spending on legitimate client communications. Like phone conversations, e-mail communications on client matters represent billable time. Yet lawyers are going so fast, doing so many things, that they don't actually write down their time notation as

When it comes to purchasing new technology, many lawyers and law firms seem to make decisions without adequate preparation— and usually without fully understanding the impact the new hardware or software will have on their firms. Before taking the leap, ask yourself the following four questions:

1. *What is the return on investment (ROI) of the purchase?*
2. *Will the new technology increase the competence of my staff and make the office more efficient?*
3. *Will the new hardware or software allow me to do something I couldn't do before?*
4. *Will the quality of my services be improved?*

If you cannot answer those questions, you are not ready to buy.

they're working on e-mails. And if they don't do it then, by the end of the day, let alone the end of the week, they will forget how much time was needed. Client e-mails get so enmeshed in what has been called "administrivia" that their importance is not adequately accounted for. The result is lost profitability.

E-mails also involve other financial costs that are not readily apparent. Based on personal experience, it is easy to estimate that most lawyers take about one to two hours each workday to "clear out" their e-mail boxes apart from getting to client matters. If we assume 200 workdays per year (there are more), and two hours per day and $200 per hour billable value for an attorney (most are charging more today), the calculation is $80,000 of wasted billable time annually. It goes without saying that this is hugely expensive.

Hiring the right person the first time for the right job will create more profits.

Case Study: The real cost of lawyer turnover

For every lawyer dismissed or leaving the law firm, there is a cost to the firm. This is "turnover cost," which has a nasty way of getting hidden but directly impacts the bottom line of a firm's financial analysis.

Consider this hypothetical example. Lawyer "A" is earning $160,000; he was hired via an executive search firm whose fee is 25% of the first year's compensation package, or in this case $40,000. Assume further that the firm is somewhat progressive and does have an education program that helps the lawyer new to the firm assimilate into the firm culture; in this case, the training time is 100 hours for the associate at his billable rate of $200 per hour, or $20,000. Don't forget the cost of the partners doing the training: 100 hours at their rate of $500 per hour, or $50,000. Assume still further that there was time spent by partners in the recruiting process and interviewing this lawyer to the tune of 50 hours at their billable rate of $500 per hour, or an additional $25,000 in costs.

Without considering additional items of reduced productivity when the lawyer new to the firm first gets started or the cost to the firm of disruption, retraining and client concern when another lawyer is assigned to a matter in the "middle

of the stream," the real cost and time value to
the firm during the first year of employment is
already $295,000. This is not a small factor ...
and at least $135,000 is repeated every time a
lawyer, irrespective of the reason, leaves the firm.
It is for this reason that law firms must evaluate
their candidates carefully. Hiring the right person
the first time for the right job will create more
profits. The most effective way to increase profits
is to hire the right people and provide extensive
education for them to improve their skills and then
purchase the technology that will enable them to
do what they need to do more efficiently. That's
PROFITABILITY!

Case Study: The real cost of capital investment

All technology investments should provide a return
to the firm. A 10% return is usually considered too
low to make the purchase (investment) unless there
are other factors involved, such as new services the
purchase allows you to offer or greater efficiency
that it gives you. There is no one right or correct
rate of return. The return selected or expected is a
function of personal choice, available alternatives,
and available resources for investment. When
you have a number of technology expenditures
competing for your attention, using ROI is a
great way to rank them in the order of financial
preference. Then, depending on the budget and
resources available, you can proceed down the list
and take the most productive or profitable first.
This analysis, besides being important for the
decision-making process, can also come into play in

financing the investment. With bank borrowing or lease financing, the provider of the capital will want to know how the purchase will impact your practice and how you plan to repay the new debt.

Be aware, however, of the other factors that affect ROI. Take the example of an attorney who had a large personnel turnover and decided to improve the productivity of the new staff by purchasing software specific to the attorney's practice. Cost of the new system and training would be $15,000, but the productivity of the staff would double, allowing for more work, fewer people and greater cash flow. The calculated net increase in savings and in profitability would amount to $30,000 in the first twelve months alone: an ROI of 200% in the first year, with a payback period (recouping the initial investment) of six months. The decision seemed easy and the purchase was made, but the ROI was thwarted by human considerations: The staff was resistant to the change, afraid of the new system, and had no emotional investment in its use. The software languished until it became obsolete, with little of the expected savings or profits.

Case Study: The real cost of telecommuting

The idea of telecommuting seems increasingly attractive to lawyers. The usual perceptions of whether this is a good idea revolve around firm policy and client expectations in terms of "face time" and accessibility. But other points, tangible and intangible, are equally important in a business context:

The personal exchange of ideas and guidance from one lawyer to another, sometimes called firm culture, are vital to a successful law firm practice.

- Lawyers often are not entitled to work from home when a physical office space is available at the firm. If office space is no longer used for at least 20% of the time, someone else must either use the space while the telecommuting attorney is absent or the firm will eat the expense and thus incur a greater cost for off-site operations.

- All practices do not lend themselves equally well to telecommuting. Transactional work typically can be done this way more readily than litigation.

- The personal exchange of ideas and guidance from one lawyer to another, sometimes called firm culture, are vital to a successful law firm practice. A lawyer's physical absence from the firm causes the culture to suffer.

- A lawyer's physical presence in a law firm is often the starting point of business judgment. Years of working in a physical law firm setting, not a virtual one, can enable a seasoned legal practitioner to walk the floor of an unfamiliar firm and get a sense of whether they're making money or not, whether they're serving the client well or not, even without knowing a thing about their practice.

Section 10:

Business Competency Resources

Smith's undergraduate degree was in history, while Jones majored in political science. Neither attorney received any kind of business training while in law school, but neither bought into the idea that actively working to create a profitable firm is "unprofessional." Smith and Jones realized, after their first year in practice, that they would benefit from a better grounding in business basics, but neither had the time for business courses or an MBA—particularly when such training doesn't apply to CLE requirements. What do they do now?

There are a variety of resources available to law firms that want to increase the business competency of their lawyers. General resources within the profession include the many programs, publications and materials of the American Bar Association (www.abanet. org) and the comprehensive online education programs found at the West Legal Education Center (www. westlegaledcenter.com), which compiles business and legal education programs of the Practicing Law Institute, National Bar Association and many others. General training

A plan is a scheme or program for making or doing something. It is a detailed method, formulated beforehand, of proceeding on a course of action. In the case of managing a law practice, a good business plan:

- *Is simple to understand*
- *Involves time and effort to create*
- *Is ongoing and evolving, being changed as circumstances change and more accurate information is gathered*
- *Is based on shared beliefs*
- *Is agreeable to and supported by all those with responsibility to act—staff as well as lawyers*

programs and materials on business competency are available through the American Management Association (www.amanet. org), The Conference Board (www.conference-board.org) and the Professional Services Management Association (www.psmanet.org).

Progressive law firms are creating business education programs for their lawyers. One of the most notable is that of Chicago-based Seyfarth Shaw, which since 2003 has sent more than 150 of its partners to a three-day custom Executive Education program at Northwestern University's Kellogg School of Management. Business schools around the country can customize similar corporate executive programs for law firm use.

An even more extensive effort was announced in 2004 by Philadelphia-based Reed Smith and The Wharton School of the University of Pennsylvania. Called

Reed Smith University, this ambitious project includes a comprehensive and innovative year-round curriculum taught firmwide by senior attorneys across five distinct schools: Leadership, Business Development, Technology, Professional Support and Law. The Wharton School hosts the program, develops the concept and curriculum for the five schools, provides its professors as academic advisors, and reviews teaching styles and methods of instructors. The university's creation of profession-specific counsel is the key, making the effort different from other joint JD/MBA programs. All kinds of creative opportunities can arise from this approach.

Creative approaches to business competency and businesslike thinking can be found in the following selected list of books. None of them focus narrowly on law firm issues. Instead they are recognized classics on the kind of innovative conceptualizing any professional can do to make an organization more successful:

- ▸ Harry Beckwith, *Selling the Invisible* (provides basic, practical strategies to improve the bottom line in any business by perceiving and fulfilling a client's every need)

- ▸ David Maister, *Managing the Professional Service Firm* (offers the classic exposition of how skilled managers combine true professionalism and bottom-line thinking)

- ▸ Jim Collins, *Good to Great* (uses rigorous research and invigorating teaching to show how even the dullest of organizations can excel)

- Jack Canfield, *Power of Focus* (gives you the success principles necessary to hit your business, financial and personal targets)

- Alan Weiss, *Million Dollar Consulting* (shows how consultants can raise capital, reel in new clients, set fees, accelerate growth, and achieve $1 million in annual revenue)

- Blaine McCormick, *Ben Franklin: America's Original Entrepreneur* (applies the bottom-line thinking of Franklin's autobiography for modern times)

The LawBiz Management Company of Edward Poll & Associates, Inc. (www.lawbiz.com) is a leading consultant organization that works with lawyers to increase their profits and their effectiveness at practicing law. Edward Poll, J.D., M.B.A., C.M.C., author of this special report, is a nationally recognized coach and adviser who gives coaching and strategic guidance to national and regional law firms and their leaders on practice management, business development, and financial matters. He has practiced law for 25 years, was the CEO and COO of several manufacturing businesses, and has been a business and profitability consultant to law firms for 15 years. He frequently writes and speaks on The Business of Law®, and his widely praised books are all detailed on and available through his Web site, www.lawbiz.com, including:

- *Attorney and Law Firm Guide to The Business of Law®: Planning and Operating for Survival and Growth* (Second Edition, American Bar Association, 2002). A comprehensive guide to all aspects of operating a law firm.

- *Collecting Your Fee: Getting Paid from Intake to Invoice* (American Bar Association, 2003). Advice on engagement letters, detailed bills, fee agreements and intake forms.

- *Law Practice Management Review: The Audio Magazine for Busy Attorneys*™. One-hour audiotapes present expert interviews on the latest law practice management techniques.

- *Profitable Law Office Handbook: Attorney's Guide to Successful Business Planning.* A best-selling, practical guide that enables attorneys to take control of their financial futures.

- *Secrets of the Business of Law: Successful Practices for Increasing Your Profits.* Specific suggestions for greater operating efficiency and profitable revenue generation.

- *Selling Your Law Practice: The Profitable Exit Strategy.* A guide to help attorneys determine the value of their practice and get top dollar for it.

"You've got to be careful if you don't know where you're going because you might not get there."

—*Yogi Berra*

Get these other informative books by Ed Poll

Attorney and Law Firm Guide to The Business of Law:
Planning and Operating for Survival and Growth
Second Edition
By Edward Poll

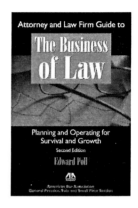

Do you want to:
* Be more successful by design than by accident?
* Be more profitable?
* Attract more clients?
* Have your clients pay on time?
* Have greater control of your practice?
* Have greater peace of mind?

If your answer is yes to any one of these questions, you must read this book. Ed Poll had simplified the mystical process of operating a law practice so anyone can be more effective with his or her clients and become more profitable.

Selling Your Law Practice:
The Profitable Exit Strategy
By Edward Poll

Get Top Dollar for Your Law Practice!

You will discover how to:
* Determine the value of your practice
* Set your sale price
* Evaluate and describe your practice's unique characteristics
* Negotiate the sale more effectively
* Anticipate transition issues
* Review state's Rules of Professional Conduct for selling a practice

The CD contains the sample contracts, forms, and financial worksheets from the book in Word and Excel format!

Call **(800) 837-5880** or **visit www.lawbiz.com** to order!